S0-BBC-035

Why didn't the Pole want to buy any pornographic materials?

(page 8)

What's "Fi fi fo, fo fo fi fo"?

(page 17)

How was break dancing invented?

(page 19)

What do you say to a Puerto Rican in a three-piece suit?

(page 24)

What's the purpose of a belly button?

(page 72)

Why do you wrap a hamster in electrician's tape?

(page 114)

Also by Blanche Knott

Blanche Knott's

Truly Tasteless Jokes IV

St. Martin's Press
New York

ST. MARTIN'S PRESS TITLES ARE AVAILABLE AT QUANTITY DISCOUNTS
FOR SALES PROMOTIONS, PREMIUMS OR FUND RAISING. SPECIAL
BOOKS OR BOOK EXCERPTS CAN ALSO BE CREATED TO FIT SPECIFIC
NEEDS. FOR INFORMATION WRITE TO SPECIAL SALES MANAGER, ST.
MARTIN'S PRESS, 175 FIFTH AVENUE, NEW YORK, N.Y. 10010.

BLANCHE KNOTT'S TRULY TASTELESS JOKES IV

Copyright © 1984 by Blanche Knott

ISBN: 0-312-90365-0
Can. ISBN: 0-312-90366-9

St. Martin's Press
175 Fifth Avenue
New York, New York 10010

Contents

Blanche Knott's

TRULY
TASTELESS
JOKES
IV

Helen Keller

Why can't Helen Keller have children?
  Because she's dead.

•

What's the most useless thing for Helen Keller to have?
  Eyes.

•

What's the second most useless thing for Helen Keller to have?
  A camera.

•

Why did Helen Keller go all the way on her first date?
  She'd never been taught to say no.

How does Helen Keller tell the difference between the ladies' room and the men's room?
  She feels her way around.

●

How did Helen Keller's mother confuse her?
  She gave her bird seed to read.

●

What's Helen Keller's favorite rock-'n'-roll theme?
  "Cum On Feel the Noize."

●

What's the cruelest thing to do to Helen Keller?
  Use a hand buzzer.

●

How do you save Helen Keller from drowning?
  Hand-to-hand resuscitation.

●

What did Helen Keller get for her birthday?
  Polio.

Polish

A Polish girl called up her druggist and asked what to do for her boyfriend's dandruff and he recommended Head & Shoulders. She called back a week later and asked, "How do you give someone shoulders?"

●

The Polish athlete was being examined before the Olympics. "Tell me," asked the doctor, "have you ever used steroids?"

The athlete replied, "Not since I switched to Preparation H."

●

Two rich Poles, Stan and Jerzy, are on a camping trip, when Jerzy says to Stan, "I have to go to the bathroom." Stan suggests he go into the bushes. Five minutes later there's a shout from the bushes: "I have nothing to wipe with!"

"Use a dollar," Stan shouts back, then holds his nose

as Jerzy emerges from the woods with his hand covered with shit. "What happened?" he asks.

"You gave me some rotten advice," complained Jerzy. "Not only am I covered with shit, I got four quarters stuck up my ass!"

●

A Pole was jumped by two muggers and fought like hell, but he was finally subdued. His attackers went through his pockets. "You mean you fought like that for fifty-seven cents?" asked one of the muggers incredulously.

"That's all you wanted?" moaned the Pole. "I thought you were after the four hundred dollars in my shoe."

●

What's black, crispy, and sits on top of the roof?
A Polish electrician.

●

After World War Two, two Poles return to their destroyed village to locate the first one's wife. Going through the rubble, Victor comes across a dismembered arm and calls over, "Hey, Stanley, wasn't this Anya's arm? I think it's the wristwatch you gave her."

"I dunno, Victor," says Stanley, and they walk on. A little farther on, Victor comes across a severed leg. "Stanley, couldn't this be part of Anya? She had great legs."

Stanley shrugs and they walk on. Finally the energetic Victor comes across a woman's head, which he holds out at arms' length for his friend's inspection.

"Nope," says Stanley at last. "Anya was much taller."

Three Polish guys go out on the town, looking for a good time. The first loses no time in picking up a cute brunette and they disappear off to her place. The second soon finds a willing redhead and they check into a motel across the street. The third eyes an attractive blonde and asks if she wants to come back to his apartment and have a wild time. "I'd love to," she says, "but I'm on my menstrual cycle."

"That's quite all right," said the Pole. "I rode my moped."

●

A Polish woman went into the drugstore and asked for a deodorant for her husband. "Certainly," said the clerk. "How about the ball type?"

"Oh, no," she said, "it's for under his arms."

●

What did the Pole say when he stuck his head into the toilet bowl?

"Howdy, doody."

●

Why did the Polish couple decide to have only four children?

Because they read in the newspaper that one out of every five babies born in the world today is Chinese.

●

Why did eighteen Poles get together to go to the same movie?

Because they read the sign UNDER SEVENTEEN NOT ADMITTED.

Did you hear about the Polish girl who had two chances to get pregnant?

She blew both of them.

•

An American, a Pole, and an Italian all hear about a legendary bridge: If you have the courage to jump off it, and the presence of mind to shout in midair what you want to become, your wish will be granted. So they make the trek to the bridge and the American says he'll be daring and jump first. Over he goes, yells "Billionaire!" and lands safely on the deck chair of his giant yacht. The Italian jumps next, shouts "An eagle!" and soars up into the heavens. The Pole runs for the edge, stubs his toe on the curb as he jumps, and yells "Oh, shit!"

•

Why don't Poles play hide and seek?

Because nobody will go look for them.

•

Hear about the Pole who thought cross-breeding was getting a little on the side?

•

Secretary: "May I use your Dictaphone?"
Polish boss: "Use your finger like everyone else."

Did you hear about the Pole who bought an A.M. radio?

It took him a month to figure out he could play it at night.

•

A Pole makes a doctor's appointment because his hemorrhoids are really bothering him. The doctor gives him some suppositories and tells him to come back in a week for a checkup. "How's it going?" he asks the patient a week later.

"I gotta tell you the truth, Doc," said the Pole. "For all the good these pills did me, I coulda shoved them up my ass."

•

Why did the old Polish lady have her tubes tied?

So she wouldn't have any more grandchildren.

•

How did the Polish mother respond when her daughter announced she was pregnant?

"Are you sure it's yours?"

•

One day, while walking down the street, a Pole stops to ask a man what time it is. "It's three o'clock" is the polite reply.

"Thank you," says the Pole. "It's funny, but I've been asking that question all day long and each time I get a different answer."

7

During World War Two, a badly wounded German soldier is transferred to a Polish medical unit stationed in the United States. Fortunately for the German, an American surgeon is placed in charge of the case. However, the soldier's wounds are so severe that gangrene sets in, and the German is told that his left arm must be amputated. The patient has no choice but to agree to surgery, but asks, "Please, if you can, parachute my amputated limb back to my motherland during your next bombing run." The American agrees to do the best he can for him under wartime conditions, and the arm is dropped over Dresden on the next mission.

A little later gangrene sets in the German's left leg. Again amputation is necessary, again the patient makes his strange request, and again the limb is dropped during a bombing run. Finally the German's right foot has to come off too. The American surgeon performs the operation and is in the process of attaching the severed limb to a parachute when the Polish chief of operations rushes in. "Don't do it!" he screams. "Can't you see the man is trying to escape?"

●

Why didn't the Pole want to buy any pornographic materials?
   The needle on his pornograph was broken.

●

A Pole was wandering through Boston's combat zone when a hooker sidled up to him and purred, "Baby, if you got twenty bucks, I've got the time."
   "Thanks," said the Pole, "but I already have a watch."

●

Did you hear about the Polish bulletproof vest?
   You get your money back if it doesn't work right.

8

It's time for a Polish guy's regular physical, and the first order of business is being weighed. Feeling self-conscious about his weight, he asks if he can take off his sweater. Then, holding it carefully away from him in one hand, he steps back on the scale.

●

Why do Polish babies have big heads?
  So they don't fall out during the bridal dance.

●

The pilot and copilot of a transcontinental flight are conversing in the cockpit when the copilot notices one of the four jet engines catching fire. "Gee, Bob, how are we going to cope with this?" he asks a bit nervously.
  "No problem. Listen." The pilot picks of the microphone and announces, "Attention, all passengers: This flight will be twenty minutes late."
  Ten minutes later, engine two quits. "Attention, all passengers: We will be forty-five minutes late."
  Pretty soon engine three conks out. "Attention, all passengers: We will be an hour and a half late."
  Two Poles in economy class look at each other and one says, "Jeez, if that last engine goes out, we'll be up here all day."

●

Two Poles emigrated to America. On their first day off the boat in New York City they spied their first hot-dog vendor in the street. "Do they eat dogs in America?" one asked his companion.
  "I dunno."
  "Well, we're going to live in America, so we must

learn to do as they do." So they each bought a hot dog wrapped up in wax paper and sat down to eat them on a nearby park bench. One Pole looked inside his wax paper, then over at the other Pole, and asked, "What part did you get?"

•

What's this?

A Polish sex organ.

•

Heard of the new Polish invention?
  It's a solar-powered flashlight.

•

An American tourist was visiting the town in Poland from which his grandparents had emigrated when he saw a big crowd by the side of the road. Curiosity got the better of him and he stopped to ask an onlooker what was going on. The fellow explained that a protester against the repression of Polish civil liberties had doused himself with gasoline and set himself on fire. "That's terrible," gasped the American. "But why is everyone still standing around?"

"Someone's taking a collection for his wife and kids," the man explained. "Would you be willing to help?"

"Well, sure," said the tourist. "I suppose I could spare a gallon or two."

●

How many Poles does it take to make chocolate chip cookies?

Four: three to make the batter and the other to peel the M & M's.

●

What's this?

A Polish monogrammed handkerchief.

●

Why do Poles buy aspirin?

They need the cotton.

●

A Pole, German, and American were driving across the country when their car broke down. They asked a nearby farmer if they could sleep in his barn. The farmer grudgingly agreed, but said, "Y'all had better be quiet, though. I don't like prowlers, and I'm likely to shoot first and ask questions later." The three men agreed not to make any noise and lay down to sleep, but eventually the American had to get up and take a leak. As he stumbled down the stairs in the dark, he heard the farmer cock his rifle and shout. "Who's that?"

"Meow," said the American, and the farmer went back to bed.

A little while later the German too felt the call of nature, but again a "Meow" calmed the jumpy farmer.

When it was the Pole's turn he got as far as the foot of the stairs before the farmer called out, "Who the hell's *that*?"

Said the Pole, "It's me, the cat."

•

A Polish guy came home early from work to find his wife lying on the bed, panting and sweaty. "Honey, I think I'm having a heart attack," she gasped. The Pole ran downstairs to call the doctor, and on the way his little son told him, "Daddy, daddy, there's a naked man in the closet."

The Pole ran back upstairs, opened the closet, pulled out his best friend, and yelled, "Jesus, Jerry, Marie's having a heart attack and here you are, scaring the kids!"

•

Did you hear about the Pole who was found unconscious in his jail cell with twelve bumps on his head?

He tried to hang himself with a rubber band.

•

How do Polish people reproduce?

They exchange underwear.

Why shouldn't you buy Polish goldfish?
  They drown.

●

Did you hear about the Polish gynecologist who used two fingers?
  He wanted a second opinion.

Black

The contestants on a television game show turned out to be an Italian, a Pole, and a black. The contest involved a spelling test, and the MC asked each in turn to spell *before*. The Italian said, "B - E - F- O -E."

The Pole said, "B - E - F - O."

The black said, "B - E - F - O - R - E."

Lights flashed and buzzers sounded as the MC congratulated the black contestant. "Now for the $10,000 grand prize," he announced, "use *before* in a sentence."

A few moments of strained silence went by until the black guy blurted out, "Two and two be fo'."

●

What do you call a black opera singer?
Ne-ga-roe! (Like Figaro. Get it?)

●

Did you hear about the thirty-year-old man from Harlem?
All his friends were dead.

What did the black kid get for Christmas?
   My bike.

•

A farmer in the Deep South was out looking over his tobacco fields when a bus full of blacks rounded a corner on the country road too fast and rolled over on its side. Losing no time, the farmer ran back to the barn for his pick and shovel, and proceeded to start burying the bus. Just as he was finishing up the job, a state police cruiser arrived on the scene. "Say, didn't a bus fulla black folks just go off the road around here?"
   "Yep," replied the farmer.
   "Well, where'd they get to?"
   "I buried 'em" was the answer.
   "Gee," said the trooper, "were they all dead?"
   The farmer looked straight at the trooper and said, "Well, some of 'em said they weren't, but you know how they lie."

•

What do blacks and Christmas trees have in common?
   They both have colored balls.

•

Why can't blacks celebrate Thanksgiving?
   Kentucky Fried Chicken isn't open on holidays.

•

What was "We 'B' Toys"'s number-one seller last Christmas?
   Cotton Patch dolls.

15

Two alligators met in the swamp. One was a giant specimen, while the other was a skinny, emaciated little animal. The runt asked, "Say, sir, how'd you get so big?"

"I eat blacks" was the big gator's answer.

"So do I," said junior, "but look at me."

"What do you do to 'em?" asked the behemoth.

"I catch 'em and beat the shit out of 'em, then down the hatch they go."

"Now, there's your mistake," drawled the monstrous alligator. "Just catch 'em and eat 'em. If ya beat the shit out of 'em, all ya got left is lip skin and sneakers."

●

Why don't sharks attack blacks?

Because they mistake them for whale shit.

●

One day a kindergarten teacher decided to test her students on animal sounds. Calling on little white Mary, she asked, "Mary, what does the cow say?"

"Moooo," answered Mary.

"Very good," said the teacher. "Now, Johnny, what does the sheep say?"

"Baaaa," replied little white Johnny.

Then the teacher asked little black Leroy, "What does the pig say, Leroy?"

Leroy thought for a moment, then said, "*Freeze*, nigger."

●

How do you circumsize a black?

Use a jigsaw.

Why do blacks call white people "honkies"?
That's the last noise they hear before the white people run them over.

•

Did you hear that they isolated the cause of sickle-cell anemia?
It's the glue on food stamps.

•

What's "Fi-fi-fo, fo-fo-fi-fo"?
The mayor of Chicago's phone number.

•

What do blacks use for jock itch?
Black Flag.

•

Why can't blacks do push-ups?
Their lips stick to the floor before their chests touch.

•

What do you call a building full of blacks?
A coon-dominium.

What's this?

The last thing a black sees after the Klan throws him down a well.

•

Little Titus was fooling around on the back porch one day and came across a can of white paint. He proceeded to paint his face and hands with it and run into the kitchen. "Look, Ma, I'm a white boy now!" he shouted.

"God*damn*, Titus, you black as the ace of spades and don't you forget it! Now go wash up before someone sees you."

Crestfallen, Titus went in search of his father, saying, "Look, Daddy, I'm a white boy now!"

"GodDAMN, boy," roars his father, "you stupid or what? Go wash that crap off before I take my belt to you!"

"You know, Daddy," says Titus, "I've only been white for five minutes or so, and already I'm beginning to hate you niggers."

•

How do you wipe out 250 black families?
   Blow up K Mart.

There was this black guy working on a roofing gang. He stopped to take a leak and the foreman shouted over to ask what he was doing. "Nuthin'," stammered the guy.

"Then drop that roll of tar paper," yelled the foreman, "and get the hell out of here."

●

Did you hear about the tonic that turns blacks into whites?
  It's called Fade, Spade.
And the antidote?
  Renege.

●

Jesse Jackson requested an audience with the Pope, and permission was granted during the pontiff's weekly excursion in his rowboat. Reverend Jackson was willing to go along with this, so the two men set out across the pond in the papal rowboat, deeply engaged in conversation. About a half an hour later they were heading back toward shore when a breeze came up and blew the Pope's hat into the water. Jackson nimbly stepped out of the boat, walked across the water to retrieve the hat, and the two eminent men returned to shore.

The next morning the press coverage of the event ran: BLACK CAN'T EVEN SWIM.

●

How was break dancing invented?
  By black kids stealing hubcaps from moving cars.

Jewish

What does the Jewish Santa Claus say as he comes down the chimney?

"Ho-ho-ho! Anybody want to buy some toys?"

•

Mr. Cohn, Mr. Katz, and Mr. Rabinowitz are such avid golfers that their wives finally get fed up with being "golf widows" and insist on a two-week vacation in Miami Beach. On pain of divorce, each promises not to even mention golf to his wife. But by the third day all three are climbing the walls, and sure enough where do they run into each other on the fourth day but the local golf course. "You wouldn't believe this, fellas," moans Cohn, "but this game is costing me, $45,000 for a new Mercedes for my wife."

"You think that's bad," says Katz, "listen to this: I gotta shell out $110,000 for a new condominium."

Rabinowitz smiles and says, "You poor schmucks, I'm here without it costing me a penny. At six A.M. I rolled over and said, 'Well, Becky, what's it going to be, golf course or intercourse?' She says, 'Take a sweater so you shouldn't catch cold.'"

How do Jews play football?
    They try to get the quarter back.

●

Why don't JAPs wear chastity belts?
    Because Jewish men like to eat locks.

●

What's the definition of a JAP?
    A girl who thinks cooking and fucking are two cities in China.

●

Three Jews are sitting on the beach in front of the Palm Beach Hilton talking about the trouble they're having with their respective business. Says Leonard, "I lost almost $50,000 when my store burned down, but thank God the furs were insured."
    Bernard says, "That's nothing. I lost $200,000 when my tailor shop was destroyed in that big flood, but I also, thank God, was insured."
    Then Chaim pipes up, "So how do you start a flood?"

●

Why do Jewish men like the cheap prostitutes in Mexico?
    Because of all the frijoles.

A woman goes into a Jewish deli and buys two loaves of raisin bread. About an hour later the phone starts ringing off the hook; the owner of the deli answers it and it's the lady shopper. "Listen," she hisses into the phone, "the raisin bread I bought from you has two cockroaches in it! Now, what are you going to do about it?"

The deli owner thinks it over, then replies, "So bring back the cockroaches, lady, and I'll give you two raisins."

●

What four-letter Jewish word means "intercourse"?
   Talk.

●

Mr. Cohen emigrated to the United States as a young man and fulfilled the immigrant's dream: He ran his own profitable nail factory in Brooklyn, bought a nice house, sent his kids to college, even put the oldest son through Harvard Business School. When the young man graduates, Mr. Cohen says to him, "Moishe, you're a smart one, and I'm going to turn the business over to you and retire to Miami Beach."

A year later he gets an excited call from Moishe. "Dad, things are going great: I've computerized inventory, automated the factory, even got a great new ad campaign. You've gotta come see with your own eyes."

So he picks Mr. Cohen up at the airport, and just before they reach the factory a huge billboard looms up. It's a close-up of Jesus on the cross, with the slogan USE COHEN'S NAILS FOR THE TOUGHEST JOBS. "Oy, Moishe," groans Mr. Cohen, "is that your new campaign? I'm telling you, the goys are never going to go for it."

A year later Moishe calls again. "Dad, you gotta come up again and see how great things are going. And by the way, you were right about that ad campaign; we've got a whole new one now." So Mr. Cohen flies up again and on the way from the airport he sees the same giant billboard. This time it's a picture of Jesus crumpled in a heap at the foot of the cross, and the slogan is YOU SHOULDA USED COHEN'S NAILS.

Ethnic Variegated

What do you say to a Puerto Rican in a three-piece suit?
  "Will the defendant please rise?"

•

Why aren't Arabs circumcised?
  So they have somewhere to put their gum in a sandstorm.

•

What does an Oriental use for a blindfold?
  Dental floss.

•

What do you call four drowning Mexicans?
  Cuatro sinko.

24

How can you tell when you're at an Australian stag party?
A sheep jumps out of the cake.

●

What's dumber than four Italians trying to build a house underwater?
Six Irishmen trying to lay the foundation.

●

If you throw a $100 bill out the window, which of the following four will catch it: Santa Claus, the Easter Bunny, a Polish man, or a smart black?
The Pole. There's no such thing as Santa Claus, the Easter Bunny, or a smart black.

●

Why aren't there any Mexican contestants in the summer Olympics?
Because everyone who can run, jump, or swim is already over here.

●

What does the bumper sticker on a WASP's car say?
Honk if you want to pass.

●

A Polish guy ties up his dog outside and goes into the corner bar for a quick one. He's followed in by a black guy, who comes over and says, "Hey, buddy, is that your dog outside?" The Pole says yes.

"Well, she's in heat," says the black.

"No she's not," says the Pole. "I'm sure I tied her up in the shade."

"Listen, has she been bred?" asks the black, trying again.

"Oh, yes, I fed her before we went out."

The black guy gives up. "Your dog needs to be fucked, pal."

"Oh, in that case, go right ahead," says the Pole politely. "I've always wanted a coon dog."

•

What do you call an Armenian with lots of girl friends?
   A shepherd.

•

What's this?

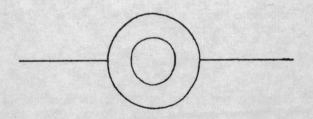

A Mexican riding a bike.

What's this?

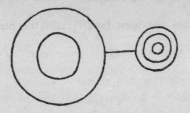

A Mexican frying an egg.

What's this?

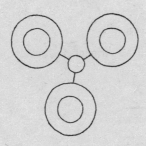

Three Mexicans pissing in a can.

•

Did you hear about the Italian who thought a vulva was an automobile from Sweden?

•

Why is Cuba so screwed up?
   It's got the island in the Caribbean, the government in Russia, the troops in Angola, and the population in Miami.

27

How do you cure a Puerto Rican of bed-wetting?
   Give him an electric blanket.

●

How do Germans tie their shoes?
   In little Nazis.

●

What do you call birth control pills in Italy?
   Wop stoppers.

●

What's this?   X
               ———
               Xski
               ———

A Pole co-signing for a black.

●

How do you get a WASP's cat out of a tree?
   Call the Fire Department.

●

What do the Chinese call 69?
   Two Can Chew.

What's it called when a Puerto Rican falls into the ocean?
  An oil slick.

●

A Chinaman walked into a bar and said to the black bartender, "I'll have a jigger, nigger."
  "You weren't trying to insult me, were you, pal?" asked the bartender. The Chinaman reassured him to the contrary. "Then let's change places," suggested the bartender. They did, and the black walked up the bar and said, "Gimme a drink, chink."
  The Chinaman replied, "Sorry, we don't serve niggers."

●

Did you hear about the Puerto Rican burglar whom the cops swore they could hear a mile away?
  He finally got wise and left his radio at home.

●

Why did they take the "911" numbers off police patrol cars?
  Mexicans kept stealing the patrol cars, thinking they were Porsches.

●

Did you hear what happened to the Puerto Rican water polo team?
  The horses drowned.

An Eskimo moves to a new community, and after finishing his igloo he goes into town to get to know his neighbors. But everyone gives him the cold shoulder until finally another Eskimo, a little friendlier than the rest, tells him it's because he hasn't taken the bravery test. "First you must drink two quarts of vodka," he explains, "then go into the polar bear's cave and kill it with your bare hands, and then all you have to do is screw an Eskimo woman outside at twenty below zero."

The newcomer realizes that if he doesn't take the test he'll never be accepted, so he proceeds to down the two quarts of vodka and go stumbling toward the cave. An hour or so later he emerges from the cave, lurches back into the bar where his friend is, and mumbles, "Now, where's that woman I gotta kill?"

•

Polish game show question: What famous place in New York State was named after blacks?
   Answer: Niggra Falls.

•

How can you tell when a Paki has matured?
   He takes the diaper off his ass and sticks it on his head.

•

There's a disturbing commercial being aired in Mexico City these days. This guy comes on the screen, flicks open a switchblade, and says, "Never leave home without your Mexican Express Card."

What do you call a Puerto Rican who only writes clean words on the wall?

An interior decorator.

●

What's it called when you hit a white man over the head?

A honkey-tonk.

●

Did you hear about the new bar for gentiles only?

It's called "Goys 'R' Us."

●

This big black guy saved all his money for years and years until one day he walked into a Cadillac showroom and put down cash for the car of his dreams, a huge maroon sedan with all the extras. Getting behind the wheel with a huge smile on his face, he called out to the salesman. "Now, tell me, how do I look?"

"Well, you asked for it," said the salesman. "Okay, I see a big buck nigger sitting in a Cadillac, happy as all get-out!"

"*Boy*, I'm glad to hear you say that. I thought you were gonna say, 'There goes another damn Guinea contractor!' "

●

What's the difference between white fairy tales and black fairy tales?

White fairy tales start out, "Once upon a time," and black fairy tales start out, "You motherfuckers ain't gonna *believe* this shit . . ."

Did you hear how the dumb Swede flunked his driver's test?

He opened the door to let out the clutch.

•

Did you hear about the new Japanese-Jewish restaurant?

It's called So-Sue-Mi.

Handicapped

What do you do when an epileptic has a fit in your bathtub?
Throw in your laundry.

●

Hear about the Polish terrorists?
They attacked the Special Olympics.

●

Did you know Disney World offers rides for the disabled?
The blind can rent seeing-eye kangaroos.

●

A man had been going to a psychiatrist for many years, and finally the doctor pronounced him cured of his mental illness. On hearing the news, the ex-patient smiled, shook the doctor's hand, and pulled out a revolver.

"What the hell are you doing?" screamed the shrink.

"Well, Doc, you've helped me a hell of a lot . . . but now you know too much!"

Where do epileptics go when in Las Vegas?
    Seizures Palace.

●

Did you hear about Martha the midget?
    She went into the bar and kissed everyone in the joint.

●

How about the amputee with cancer?
    He had one stump in the grave.

●

How do crazy people go through the forest?
    They take the psycho path.

●

What's the definition of bad acne?
    When you walk into a Papa Gino's and the counter girl
asks you if you're to go.

●

Bumper sticker: *Roses are red,*
                Violets are blue;
                I'm schizophrenic.
                And so am I.

What do you call an epileptic in an oven?
   Shake 'n Bake.

•

Did you hear about the one-legged lady who got raped?
   She couldn't cross her legs to save her ass.

•

Who's the quadriplegic under the car?
   Jack.
And the one in the fireplace?
   Bernie.

•

What do you call a black quadriplegic in the ocean?
   Kareem Abdul Sandbar.

•

What do you call a guy with no arms or legs in the mailbox?
   Bill.
The same guy in a spice rack?
   Herb. Or Basil.

The same guy on a roll?
   Frank.

The same guy covered with oil?
   Derek.

The same guy, who always gets dumped on?
   John.

The same guy, who always gets dumped on, in England?
   Lou.

What do you call a girl with no arms and no legs going
down a river?
   Flo.

The same girl on a fence?
   Barb.

The same girl on roller skates?
   Dolly.

Okay, what do you call a guy with no arms or legs
halfway down Tina Turner's throat?
   Mike.

The same guy halfway down Liberace's throat?
   Dick.

What do you call two guys with no arms or legs hanging
on a wall?
   Kurt 'n' Rod.

What do you call a guy with no arms and legs and with a
speech impediment in the sink?
   Dwayne.

And what do you call a quadruple amputee with a
scratched-up face?
   Claude.

●

What's the difference between Quasimodo and a messy
room?
   You can straighten up a messy room.

Two harelips, Willy and Joe, just finished up two hard weeks' work on a Kansas farm. Seeing as it was payday, they got all slickered up and decided to blow some of it on a night on the town. On the way into town, Willy, the brains of the pair, began discussing plans for the night. "Lnet nit lnaid," he suggested.

"O-nay," chimed in Joe, eyes lighting up.

After a little further thought, Willy reflected, "Ya know, we'ren not gunna nit no regner girwols winth these harwips. Lnet's not mess arown, lnet's nit some whors."

"O-nay," said Joe happily.

"We better nit us some wubbers. Don' want some whors to nive us the dwip." So Joe was dispatched into the pharmacy with fifty cents. "Huh?" said the acned teenager behind the desk in answer to the request. "Wubbers, you know, are-you-be-be-ee-are-wes, wubbers!" said Joe.

"Gee, I'm sorry fella, I must not be hearing right," said the clerk, and an embarrassed Joe returned empty-handed to the car. "O-nay," said Willy after much thought, "you go back in there 'n you snay weal swolly: 'I wnant some pwo-fil-act-wics.' Snay it weal swol 'n enpaswize eah swilable." Off went Joe, only to return again, dejected and empty-handed.

"All white, Joe," proposed Willy, "now you do exactwy what I tell you to do. You go in nere 'n you unzwip your pnants 'n you way fitty tents on the countner 'n den you way your dick up nere, too, 'n he should gnet the idea." Joe marched into the store but burst out a few moments later, in tears and so frustrated that it took Willy nearly ten minutes to get the story out of him.

Tearfully, Joe began. "Willy, damwit, I did ex-actwy what you tol' me to do. I walked in nere, I waid fitty tents on the counter, I waid my dick up nere, too, and you know what he did?"

"What?" asked the anxious Willy.

"Well, he unzwipped his pnants, waid his dick on the countner, 'n his dick was two ninches longer than my dick 'n he took my fitty tents."

Lepers

Why is it illegal to tell jokes in a leper colony?
    They might laugh their heads off.

●

Why didn't the leper cross the road?
    He lost his nerves.

●

How can you tell when a leper has been in your shower?
    Your bar of soap has grown.

●

Why did the leper baseball player go blind?
    He kept his eye on the ball.

Why was the leper so embarrassed?
He struck his foot in his mouth.

●

Why was there time out at the lepers' football game?
There was a hand off at the line of scrimmage.

●

Why did the leper flunk his driver's test?
He left his foot on the gas.

●

Why did the leper go back into the shower?
He forgot his head and shoulders.

●

Why did they stop the leper baseball game?
Someone dropped a ball in left field.

Celebrities

Who killed David Kennedy?
  Syringe Syringe.

•

Why was Jesse Jackson so successful in retrieving the POW from Syria?
  Colored folks always *were* good at fetchin'.

•

Why does Dolly Parton have to buy her bras at the Datsun dealership?
  So she can get a 280Z.

•

Did you hear about the one-inch-high Marie Osmond doll?
  It's so cherry, they put it on top of banana splits.

Fidel Castro was addressing a huge crowd in Havana: "They accuse me of intervening in Angola . . ." and a voice in the crowd cried loudly, "Peanuts! Popcorn!" Castro resumed: "They say I've intervened in Mozambique . . ." and was again interrupted by the cry of "Peanuts! Popcorn!" Picking up a third time, Castro went on: "They tell me I'm intervening in Nicaragua . . ." and once more the vendor yelled, "Peanuts! Popcorn!"

Losing his temper, Castro snapped, "If that capitalist bastard yells, 'Peanuts! Popcorn!' once more, I'll kick his ass all the way to Miami!"

The entire audience screamed, "PEANUTS! POPCORN!"

•

Did you hear that Natalie Wood and Linda Lovelace are teaming up on a new movie?

It's going to be called *Deep Float*.

•

Did you hear about Liz Taylor's new soap opera?
All My Chins.

•

What's the difference between Elizabeth Taylor and a Guernsey cow?

Fifteen pounds and eight husbands.

•

Did you know Dennis Wilson opened the Endless Summer Diving School?

41

What type of racquet doesn't float?
A Wilson.

●

What did Wendy say when she stuck her hand down Ronald McDonald's pants?
"Where's the beef?"

●

Why did Alex Haley try to commit suicide?
He found out he was adopted.

●

What do you call a baby tennis player?
Fetus Gerulaitis.

●

Why was Jessica Savitch unable to swim to safety?
Because she was an anchorwoman.

●

What was her favorite perfume?
Canal No. 5.

●

What has three balls and comes from outer space?
E.T.—the Extra Testicle.

42

Did you hear about the souvenir campaign buttons from the Mondale-Ferraro ticket?
  They say, "Vote for Wally and the Beaver."

●

What were the last words Marvin Gaye's father said to him?
  "This is the last 45 you'll ever hear."

●

How did Marvin Gaye die?
  He heard it through the carbine.

●

Heard about the new Detroit record label?
  It's called "Mowdown."

●

Did you hear that the runner-up Miss America had to resign the crown too?
  They found naked pictures of her parents in *National Geographic*.

●

When Tarzan first met Jane, he said, "What name?"
  "Jane."
"What whole name?"
  "Cunt."

Did you hear about Jesse Jackson's plan to eliminate unemployment?

He's expanding the NBA to 5,000 teams.

●

When Jesse Jackson was asked about the new abortion bill, he said, "Ah thought ah paid it . . ."

●

What happened when John Landis didn't like the setup on *Twilight Zone*?

Heads rolled!

●

You heard about Michael Jackson and Richard Pryor's new charity?

The Ignited Negro College Fund.

●

What's the Fund's motto?

"The mind is a terrible thing to baste."

●

What's black and flaming and squeaks on one side and swears on the other?

Michael Jackson and Richard Pryor back-to-back.

What's this? (Hold five matches spread apart in your hand.
Light one.)
    The Jackson Five.

•

What do a Nestle's Crunch bar, Kentucky Fried Chicken,
and Michael Jackson have in common?
    They're all black and crispy.

•

Hear about the new shampoo Michael Jackson's endorsing?
    It's called Head & Smoulders.

•

What happened when Michael Jackson invited Billy Squier
and Kiss over to spend Saturday night?
    Michael beat it, Billy stroked it, and Kiss licked it up.

•

What were John Belushi's last words?
    "No Pepsi—Coke."

•

What do you call it when Dolly Parton does the backstroke?
    Islands in the Stream.

What has 500 pounds of hair and can't get through a revolving door?
   Dolly Parton.

●

Did you hear that Boy George and Michael Jackson are sisters?
   Their parents are Joan Rivers and Mr. T!

●

Then there's the theory that Boy George is Brooke Shields on steroids.

●

One day Boy George got some good news and some bad news. The bad news was that his girl friend had left him. The good news was that all her dresses fit him.

●

Why are the Democrats consulting with Jane Wyman?
   Because she knows how to screw Reagan and then dump him.

●

Why didn't Karen Carpenter visit pool halls a lot?
   She didn't like it when people chalked her head.

Why did Richard Carpenter have such a hard time selling Karen's house?
  No kitchen.

•

Why wasn't Karen Carpenter a very good conversationalist?
  Because she never chewed the fat.

•

What does Liz Taylor have now that she's always wanted?
  A stiff Dick.

•

What was Karen Carpenter's favorite saying?
  ''Gag me with a spoon.''

•

What's Roman Polanski's latest movie?
  Close Encounters with the Third Grade.

•

What's John Lennon doing these days?
  Decomposing.

What did Bob Wagner say to Natalie Wood before they left for the party?

"Have a few drinks, but don't go overboard."

•

Know how Tarzan got his famous yell?

He found Jane surrounded by a tribe of hungry cannibals. Grabbing a handy vine, he swung down to her rescue, shouting, "Jane, grab the vine. No, Jane, the vine, the *vine* . . . Aa aahaahaaaa!"

•

How did Karen Carpenter die?

She was killed in a crash diet.

•

What did Karen Carpenter's mother keep saying to her?

"Stop singing at the table and eat!"

•

What's the difference between Joan Collins and the *Titanic*?

Only fifteen hundred went down on the *Titanic*.

•

What did Joan Collins say to King Kong?

"Is it in yet?"

Cruelty To Animals

A Polish biology professor was conducting research on the nervous system of the frog. Taking a frog out of the tank and putting it on the table, he said, "Jump!" The frog jumped.

Taking a scalpel, he amputated one of the frog's front legs. "Jump!" he shouted. The frog jumped.

He amputated a hind leg. "Jump!" The frog managed a respectable jump.

Amputating a third limb, the professor repeated his command. Bleeding profusely by now, the frog managed a feeble bounce.

Taking his scalpel to the fourth leg, the professor said, "Jump!" No response from the frog. "I said *jump!*" shouted the professor. The frog didn't move. "JUMP!" he bellowed in the ear of the inert animal. No movement whatsoever, and finally the scientist gave up, considering the experiment at an end.

Taking his notebook from the shelf, the Polish scientist carefully noted, "When all limbs are amputated, it is observed that the frog goes deaf."

What has a hundred balls and fucks rabbits?
   A shotgun.

●

Seen the new bumper sticker?
   SAVE THE WHALES. CLUB A SEAL INSTEAD.

●

Why doesn't Smokey the Bear have any children?
   Because every time his wife gets hot, he hits her over the head with a shovel.

●

What do you call a canary in La Machine?
   Shredded tweet.

●

A not-very-successful circus trainer was finally left with no job, no house—in fact, nothing to his name but an old bull elephant. Figuring he had to make some money out of the beast somehow, he moved over to an empty lot and started charging a dollar per person for the chance to make his elephant jump completely off the ground, offering a $500 prize to whoever succeeded. No one came anywhere close to picking up the prize money until a little kid with a baseball bat showed up one day.
   The trainer didn't want to take money off a kid and tried

to dissuade him from trying, but the boy insisted on handing over his dollar. Walking over behind the elephant, he hit it in the balls with his bat as hard as he could, and sure enough the animal went up like a rocket. And off went the little boy with $500 in his back pocket.

Desperate for a way to get his money back, the trainer started a new offer: $1000 for anyone who could make the elephant wave his trunk from side to side instead of up and down. Everything was going well until the same kid showed up again, handed over his dollar, and walked over to the elephant. "Remember me?" he asked. The elephant's trunk went up and down.

"Want me to get my bat?"

Side to side went the elephant's head vigorously, and the kid walked off with the thousand dollars.

●

What venereal disease do rabbits get?
   V.W.

●

What did the termite say when he walked into the nightclub?
   "Is the bar tender here?"

●

Desperate because her husband hadn't made love to her in months, a lonely housewife finally mustered her courage and went to their doctor for advice. The doctor was very sympathetic and wrote out a prescription for pills that were guaranteed to rekindle the husband's ardor in a big way. "They'll make him horny as hell," the doctor confided, "but they're very potent, so just put one in whatever he's drinking."

Upon arriving home, the woman left the pills on the kitchen counter and dashed off to the supermarket. It didn't take long before the cat jumped up, knocked them over onto the floor, and ate a couple, as did the family dog. And when the husband got home with a headache, he took a few, thinking they were aspirin.

When the housewife returned, she was horrified to see the dog humping the cat and the cat jumping all over the dog, but even stranger was the sight of her husband with his penis inside the pencil sharpener on the counter. "What in heaven's name are you doing, Fred?" she cried.

"See that mosquito?" he said.

•

What are the three reasons why sex is better with sheep?
   They're always in the mood.
   They never have a headache.
   When you're through screwing them, you can eat them.

•

The Smiths were very proud of their parrot, which was so intelligent that it could instantly repeat anything said to it. This was an especially big hit when they entertained, as the parrot would perch on the piano and announce the names of the arriving guests.

The only problem with the parrot was that he couldn't stay clear of the neighbor's prize chickens. The first time the neighbor caught him on top of one of the hens, he was returned with a stern warning; the next time he was confined to his perch for a week; but nothing worked. Caught in the act yet again, the parrot was punished by having all the feathers on his head shaved off.

The very next evening the Smiths were entertaining, and

the parrot took his customary position on the piano. The first couple arrived, the hostess whispered to the bird, "The Murphys," and the bird spoke up, "Announcing the Murphys." All went according to schedule and the last guests were trickling in, when the door opened to admit the hostess's father-in-law, elderly and extremely bald. Before Mrs. Smith had a chance to cue him, the bird trumpeted, "Announcing the Chicken Fuckers!"

●

What do you do when an elephant comes in your window?
  Swim for your life.

●

How can you make your turtle fast?
  Don't feed him.

●

This young woman was very fond of her pet parrot but finally could no longer put up with one of its very embarrassing habits: Whenever she would return to her apartment with a man, the bird would screech, "Someone's gonna get some tonight!" So she took it in to the vet to see whether he could recommend any treatment.

The vet explained that it was simply a question of the bird being lonely and in need of female companionship, so the next stop was the pet shop. "I'm afraid we're out of parrots at the moment," said the clerk, "but in the meantime, why don't you take home this nice lady owl and see how they get along."

A few nights later the young woman came back to the apartment with a handsome new acquaintance, but no sooner had the door opened than the parrot shrieked, "Someone's gonna get some tonight!"

"Whoooo?" hooted the owl.

The parrot glared at the owl. "Not *you*, you big-eyed bitch!"

●

How do you know it's really cold out?

Your dog sticks to the fire hydrant.

●

A mouse was sniffing around in a meadow, when an eagle swooped down, swallowed him whole, and rose up in the air again. The mouse worked his way through until his head was sticking out of the bird's asshole. "Say, buddy," he squeaked, "how high up are we, anyway?"

"Oh, about two thousand feet," answered the eagle.

"You wouldn't shit me, would you?"

●

Once upon a time there was a little girl named Little Red Riding Hood. One fine morning she set out for Grandma's house, so she put a freshly baked cake and a .357 Magnum into her basket and set off through the forest. But what should she find when she got to Grandma's but a big black wolf in the bed, who jumped up, grabbed her and snarled, "I'm going to bang you till the sun goes down."

So Little Red Riding Hood pulled out the .357 and said, "Oh, no you're not. You're going to eat me like the story says."

Once upon a time there was a little girl named Little Red Riding Hood. One fine morning she set out for Grandma's house in her new bonnet and with a freshly baked cake in her basket. But what should she find when she got to grandma's but a big bad wolf hiding out in Grandma's bed. The wolf jumped up, grabbed Little Red Riding Hood, and snarled, "You've had it, little girl. I'm going to eat you right up."

"Eat, eat, eat," cried Little Red Riding Hood, tearing off her bonnet. "Doesn't anyone *fuck* anymore?"

●

A newly recruited French Legionnaire found himself stationed in a remote fort in the desert. After a few weeks had gone by, he took one of the old-timers aside and asked what the men did for a good time. "We use a camel" was the taciturn reply. Revolted, the young soldier turned his thoughts elsewhere, but as time went by and he got hornier and hornier, he could think of little else. Taking aside another veteran soldier, he asked the same question and got the same answer: "We use the camel." Finally, desperate, the young man accepted the fact that the camel was the only available outlet, and one night he snuck out to the barn. As luck would have it, one of the old-timers happened by the barn around the same time and caught sight of the young soldier up on a crate, screwing the camel. "What the hell are you doing?" he called out.

Rather puzzled, the recruit said, "I thought you said you used the camel for a good time."

"Yes, but usually we just ride him into town."

●

A journalist found himself sent to an even more remote desert encampment to do a story on the Spartan life of these tough desert fighters. Observing that there was no town, not even an oasis, for hundreds of miles, he couldn't resist asking the drill sergeant what the men do when their sexual urges get the better of them.

"We do have camels, you know" was the answer.

"Gee, that's an awfully long ride to town," commented the journalist.

"That's not exactly the plan," said the sergeant. "You'll see in a minute." And pretty soon over a sand dune appeared a herd of frantic camels being furiously pursued by an entire battalion of soldiers with their pants around their knees. Unable to believe his eyes, the journalist gasped, "No . . . It can't be. You mean they're in that much of a hurry just to screw a camel?"

To this the sergeant, unbuckling his khakis, replied, "You wouldn't want to be left with an ugly one, would you?"

•

What do you get when you cross a skin doctor and an elephant?

A pachydermatologist.

•

Very concerned because his hens were laying fewer and fewer eggs each week, a farmer finally pinpointed the blame on his aging rooster, who clearly wasn't fulfilling his henhouse responsibilities. So he went out and bought a studly young rooster. Eyeing the newcomer, the old rooster said, "Listen, let's make a deal: I'll just take three hens, move over to that far corner, and leave all the rest to you."

"Not a chance," said the youngster. "This is my henhouse now and all the broads are mine."

"Very well," said the old rooster humbly, "but perhaps you'd do me one small favor to save my pride. Let's have a race and the winner gets the henhouse; that way it won't look as though I'm being replaced because I can't perform anymore."

Sizing up his rickety competitor, the young cock agreed, even granting him a four-length handicap. Off they started around the course, but it soon became evident that the four-length lead wasn't going to hold for long. Pretty soon it was down to two lengths, and as they rounded the turn, going flat out, the youngster was just about to overtake the old rooster. Just then the farmer stepped out onto his porch, grabbed his shotgun, and blasted the new bird into smithereens. "Dammit!" he said as he set the gun down, "That's the third gay rooster I've bought this month."

●

What do you get when you kiss a bird?
   Chirpies. It's a canarial disease that's untweetable.

●

How do you catch a unique rabbit?
   U-nique up on it.

●

(Note: This joke requires appropriate sounds and gestures by the joke-teller.)
How do you make a dog sound like a cat?
   (1) Put it in the freezer for a couple of weeks.
   (2) Take it out of the freezer and run down to the

lumberyard before it has a chance to thaw. (Here's where the sounds and gestures come in: Hold your hands as though you were operating a circular saw and make the catlike falsetto screech that resembles the sound of a circular saw going through a stubborn piece of wood.)

How do you make a cat sound like a dog?
(1) Douse the cat with gasoline.
(2) Stand back with a pack of matches. (Now take a step backward, pretend to strike a match and throw it at the imaginary cat, and make a sound—*"WOOF!"*—of a cat catching on fire.)

●

A retired schoolteacher finally realized she was tired of living alone and wanted some companionship, so after a good deal of thought she decided to visit the local pet shop. The owner suggested a parrot, with which she could conduct a civilized conversation. This seemed an excellent idea, so she bought a handsome parrot, sat him on a perch in her living room, and said, "Say 'Pretty boy.' " Silence from the bird. "Come on, now, say 'Pretty boy . . . pretty boy.' "

At long last, disgustedly, the bird said, "Oh, shit."

Shocked, the schoolteacher said, "Just for that, you get five minutes in the refrigerator." Five minutes later she put the shivering bird back on its perch and said, "Now let's hear it: 'Pretty boy . . . pretty boy.' "

"Lay off for Christ's sake, would ya, lady?" said the parrot.

Outraged, the woman grabbed the bird, said, "That's it! Ten minutes in the freezer," and slammed the door on him.

Hopping about to keep warm, what does the parrot come across but a frozen turkey waiting for Thanksgiving. Startled, he squawks, "My God, you must have told the bitch to go fuck herself!"

Why can't the scientists figure out what causes AIDS?
  They can't train the laboratory rats to butt-fuck.

●

This guy goes to the hospital and is diagnosed as having a tapeworm. "They're not easy to get rid of," says the doctor, who tells the guy to come in every day for two weeks, bringing a lemon cookie and a hard-boiled egg. Grimacing, the patient agrees, and shows up on time the next morning. To his horror, the doctor shoves the egg up the guy's asshole, then follows it with the crumbled-up lemon cookie. This goes on for twelve more days, after which the doctor tells him to come in the next day with a hard-boiled egg and a hammer. On the last day the patient drops his pants, the doctor shoves in the egg, and waits. A few minutes later the worm pokes his head out, demands, "Where the hell's my cookie?" and *wham*—that's the end of the worm.

●

If you find H_2O inside a fire hydrant, what do you find outside?
  K9P.

●

Why did the monkey fall out of the tree?
  It was dead.
Why did the chicken fall out of the tree?
  It was stapled to the monkey.

One day a mouse was driving along the road in his Mercedes when he heard an anguished roaring noise coming from the side of the road. Stopping the car, he got out and discovered a lion stuck in a deep ditch and roaring for help. Reassuring the lion, the mouse tied a rope around the axle of the Mercedes, threw the other end down to the lion, and pulled the beast out of the ditch. The lion thanked the mouse profusely and they went their separate ways.

Two weeks later the lion was out for a stroll in the country when he heard a panicked squeaking coming from the side of the road. Investigating the noise, what should he come across but the mouse stuck in the same hole. "Oh, please help me, Mr. Lion," squeaked the terrified mouse. "I saved you with my car once, remember?"

"Course I'll help you, little feller," roared the lion. "I'll just lower my dick down to you, you hold on to it, and we'll have you out of there in a jiffy." Sure enough, a few minutes later the mouse was high and dry on the roadside, trying to convey his eternal gratitude to the lion.

"Don't give it another thought," said the lion kindly. "It just goes to show that if you've got a big dick, you don't need a Mercedes."

Male Anatomy

A man is strolling on the beach when he comes across a lamp lying in the sand. He rubs it and, sure enough, a genie pops out. "I will grant you your one true desire," booms the huge, turbaned figure.

"Wow, that's really great!" exclaims the man. "I wish my dick touched the ground."

So the genie cut his legs off.

●

Why is life like a penis?

Because when it's soft it's hard to beat, but when it's hard you get screwed.

●

Being a virgin, Bob was very nervous about his upcoming wedding night, so he decided to talk it over with his friend John, who was quite a man about town. "Relax, Bob," counseled John, "you grew up on a farm: Just do like the dogs do."

61

After the honeymoon the bride stormed over to her mother's house and announced that she's never going to live with Bob again. "He's totally disgusting," she wailed to her mother. Her mother asked what the problem was, and just what it was he did that was so disgusting. The bride blushed and refused to tell, but finally broke down. "Ma, he doesn't know how to make love at all. . . . He just keeps smelling my ass and pissing on the bedpost!"

•

What's a 68?
That's when she goes down on you and you owe her one.

•

Why do Texan girls walk bowlegged?
Everything's big in Texas!

•

A salesman who is on the road is staying in a futuristic motel. He has an important sales call the next morning, and realizing he needs a trim, he calls the desk clerk to inquire whether there was a barber on the premises. "I'm afraid not, sir," said the clerk, "but down the hall there's a bank of vending machines and one will give you a haircut." Thoroughly intrigued, the salesman finds the machine, inserts fifty cents, and sticks his head in the opening. The machine starts buzzing and whirring. Fifteen seconds later he pulls out his head and discovers he's got the best haircut he's ever had.

Two feet away is another machine that says MANICURES 50¢, and the salesman thinks, Why not? So he pays the money, inserts his hands into the slot, and out they come with a terrific manicure.

The next machine has a big sign: THIS MACHINE DOES WHAT MEN NEED MOST WHEN AWAY FROM THEIR WIVES. The salesman looks both ways, unzips his fly, inserts his dick, and puts in the fifty cents. The machine buzzes away as the guy screams in excruciating pain. Fifteen seconds later it stops and he pulls it out with trembling hands: There's a button sewed to the tip.

•

A guy went into the corner drugstore and confided that two lovely young stewardesses were coming to spend the whole weekend at his apartment. "I need something to get it hard and keep it hard for the whole two days, pal." The druggist insisted that he couldn't dispense any such drug without a prescription, but after a long and detailed inventory of the stewardesses' charms, he relented and gave the guy a little bottle. "Use it sparingly," the druggist cautioned. "It's very strong stuff."

When he opened the drugstore on Monday morning, the druggist was horrified to see the guy crawling toward him on the sidewalk, bloody and battered, his clothes in tatters. As he reached the door, he whispered, "Please, doc, you've gotta get me some Ben-Gay."

"Christ, man," said the druggist, "you can't put Ben-Gay on your pecker. You'll die from the pain!"

The guy gasped, "It's not for my pecker, it's for my elbow: The stewardesses never showed up!"

•

A college professor was notorious for getting off the subject and onto his favorite topic: the evils of marijuana. Off he went one day into the inventory of horrors. "Used regularly, pot can cause lung cancer, psychic disorientation, sterility, castration . . ."

"*Wait* a minute," protested a male student. "*Castration?*"

"You bet, son," said the professor. "Just suppose your girlfriend gets the munchies."

•

Two winos, Rick and Billy, woke up in an alley in dire need of a drink but with only sixty cents between them. "Shay, I got an idea," said Rick. He used the money to purchase a hot dog from the corner vendor, then pulled Billy after him into the nearest bar and ordered a round of drinks. After downing them, seeing the bartender heading their way with the bill, Rick quickly inserted the hot dog in Billy's fly and began to suck on the end of it. "Get the hell out of here you goddamn fags!" This worked equally well at the next bar, and the next, and the next—in fact, all through the day—when they finally crawled back to their spot in the alley, dead drunk. "Ya shee what you can do with a hot dog?" slurred Rick cheerfully.

"What hot dog?" laughed Billy. "We losht the hot dog after the third bar."

•

Why do boys run faster than girls?

They have two ball bearings and a stick shift.

•

A man stops into this little backwoods restaurant for lunch, and after finishing his meals he inquires the way to the rest room. Told that it's around the back of the building he heads through the back door, finds the outhouse, and takes a shit, only to discover there's no toilet paper. But there is a sign on the wall that reads, WIPE YOURSELF WITH YOUR FINGER, THEN INSERT THE FINGER INTO THIS HOLE, AND YOUR FINGER WILL BE CLEANED WITH GREAT ATTENTION. So the man wipes up and sticks his finger through the hole.

On the other side is standing a little boy holding a brick in either hand, who claps them together at the sight of the finger poking through. The guy screams in pain, yanks his hand back, and starts sucking on his finger.

●

Why can't Gypsies have children?
Because their husbands have crystal balls.

●

This fellow had been assured by his fiancée that she was a virgin, but given the state of modern morals, he didn't completely trust her. So on their wedding night he had a little trick question ready for her. Pulling down his pajamas and revealing his dick, he asked, "Now, honey, do you know what this is?"

"That's a wee-wee," she answered coyly.

Very pleased with her naiveté, he said gently, "No, honey, it's a penis."

"Uh-uh, it's a wee-wee," she insisted, shaking her head.

A little annoyed, he said, "You've got to learn a few things, dear. Now, this is a penis."

"It can't be," she retorted. "It's not half as big as some of the penises I've seen."

●

Mr. Jones went to the sex therapist as a last resort, confiding in him that his sex life at home was terrible. The doctor leaned back in his big leather chair and said, "I advise having a few martinis first to sort of loosen things up; then let your mind roam over how exciting the whole business of sex used to be." They glanced out the window, where two dogs happened to be banging away with great abandon in the yard. "Now, look at the excitement and vitality of those animals," said the doctor. "Go home, have a few martinis, and think about the spontaneity of those dogs out in the yard. Then come back and see me in two weeks."

Two weeks later the doctor asked, "Well, how'd it go?"

"Terrible," said the patient. "It took seven martinis just to get her out in the yard."

●

What has 196 teeth and holds back a monster?
   My zipper.

●

This American tourist in Spain walks into one of the local restaurants and sits down to look over the menu. It's all in Spanish, though, so he looks around and sees a man sitting at the table next to him eating these two *huge* bull's balls. They look kind of interesting, so when the waiter asks him if he's ready to order, he says, "Yes, could I have the same thing as the fellow sitting next to me?"

"I'm sorry, *señor*, but that dish must be ordered a day in advance," the waiter tells him.

So the tourist places his order and comes back the next night ready for a feast. When the waiter serves him a plate on which are placed two tiny balls, he splutters, "What the hell's this? It's not what I saw last night!"

The waiter replies, "I'm sorry, *señor*, but sometimes the *bull* wins."

●

How did Captain Hook die?
  Jock itch.

●

What did the doctor say to the nervous patient in the waiting room about his upcoming circumcision?
  "It won't be long now."

●

A well-dressed man walked into a nice bar in the small town. Ordering two martinis, he drank one down, then poured the second on his hand. Unable to contain his curiosity, the bartender leaned over and said, "I hope you don't mind me asking, sir, but why did you waste a good drink?"
  The man replied, "I just want to get my date drunk."

●

During his monthly visit to the corner barbershop, this guy asked his barber if he had any advice about how to treat his growing baldness. After a small silence the barber leaned over and confided that the best thing he'd come across was, er, female juices.
  "But you're balder than I am!" protested the guy.
  "True," said the barber, "but you've gotta admit, I've got one hell of a mustache."

Did you hear about the man who tried to commit suicide by jumping off the Empire State Building—and lived?

He had a "light fall" suit on.

•

A couple decided to give their son a briss, but the rabbi quoted them a fee of $135. "Too much," they said, and went to another rabbi, who wanted $125. "Too much," they said, and decided to do it themselves, so they got out a big sharp knife. Two minutes later, they said, "Too much."

•

An extremely obese man shows up at his doctor's office and claims that he's tried every possible way to lose weight, to no avail. So the doctor proposes a radical diet: rectal feeding. Reassuring the fattie that he won't starve to death, the doctor explains that he can actually take in enough nutrients through the rectal walls to sustain life, but that he's sure to lose weight in the process.

Three weeks later the patient comes in for a follow-up appointment, and he's down from 360 to a trim 175 pounds. The doctor shows him into his office and asks him how he's feeling, noticing that he's bouncing up and down in his seat quite energetically. "I'm feeling great, doc; never felt better" is the reply.

"In that case, why are you bouncing up and down like that?" asked the doctor.

"Just chewing some gum!"

•

Three men stopped at a big house in the country to ask for a room for the night. When their hostess showed them to their rooms, she had one request: that they not look inside a big closet on the landing. The men resisted the temptation all night, but in the morning they opened the doors. Their hostess found them staring at a collection of hundreds of penises nailed to the doors and walls of the closet. "Well men, you asked for it," she said, then asked the first one, "What does your dad do?"

"My dad's a butcher," he stammered.

The woman took a meat cleaver and chopped off the first guy's dick and nailed it to the wall. "And what does your father do?" she asked the second man.

"My father's a carpenter," he quavered.

So the hostess took a jigsaw, cut off his cock, and nailed it to the wall. "And your dad?" she asks the third guy.

"Well, my dad's a lollipop manufacturer: You're going to have to suck mine off."

•

Once upon a time, King Arthur was preparing for a long campaign. Wanting to make sure the lovely Guinevere was safe from temptation, the king had her fitted with an ingenious chastity belt designed to amputate anything attempting penetration. Returning victorious from the battlefield six months later, the suspicious ruler ordered all the palace retainers to strip off their pants in the courtyard. One by one, Arthur saw stumps where their penises had been, except for one fellow at the end of the line. "One amongst you at least is a man strong enough to resist temptation: a man of honor," he cried. "What is your name?"

"Aaaghkuggh."

•

Female Anatomy

How many men does it take to mop a floor?
    None. It's a woman's job.

●

These two men coming home from work meet on the commuter train and get to talking. They move on from sports and the weather to the subject of their wives. Says Fred, "You should know that my wife is actually pretty ugly."

"She may not be a beauty," concedes Phil, "but my wife is probably the ugliest woman on the face of the earth."

They argue back and forth about whose wife is uglier until Fred resolves the dispute. "You come over to my house, Phil, and meet my wife. If you still think your wife is uglier, we'll go over to your house to check her out." So they go to the first man's house, have a drink with his wife, and then step outside. "Well?" asks Fred.

"I've got to admit that your wife is ugly, but mine has her beat cold," says Phil. So they go to Phil's house. Fred is highly skeptical. Upon entering through the back door,

Phil bends over, slides open a trapdoor, and yells, "Honey, come on up."

She shouts back, "Do you want me to put the bag over my head?"

"No," he shouts back down, "I don't want to screw you, I just want to show you to somebody."

●

What's this?

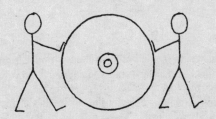

Two men walking abreast.

●

A guy and a girl are going at it hot and heavy in the backseat of his car. "Put a finger inside me," she moans. "Now two . . . Now three . . ." and so on until his whole hand is inside her. Pretty soon, following her passionate instructions, both hands are inside, and she whispers, "Put your head in." He obliges and barely hears, "Crawl in."

So he's walking around in there, when he's startled by a voice in the darkness saying "Who's there?" Another guy comes up out of the shadows and says, "What are *you* doing in here?"

"Just looking around," says the second guy.

"Well, if you find some keys, hand 'em over and we can drive my truck out of here."

What do hookers and mayonnaise have in common?
They both spread for bread.

●

The new substitute teacher was introducing herself to the class. "My name is Miss Prussy. That's like *pussycat* only with an *r*." The next morning she began class by asking if anyone remembered her name. Little Johnny's hand shot up from the third row. "Yes, you're Miss Crunt."

●

A woman walks into a bar with a duck under her arm. One of the drunks at the bar turns and says, "That has got to be the ugliest pig I've ever seen."
The woman says, "That's not a pig, it's a duck."
The drunk answers, "I was talking to the duck."

●

Heard about the flaky geneticist in southern California?
He's trying to cross a Mexican jumping bean with a cucumber in order to create the world's first organic vibrator.

●

What's the purpose of a belly button?
It's a place to put your gum in on the way down.

●

Some friends decide to help out a buddy who is still a virgin and very naive about sex. They hire an obliging prostitute for their friend for the afternoon, unaware that she's had chili for lunch. Because the guy is so naive, she suggests some "69" to start. While they're going down on each other, she can't hold in a giant, pungent fart. A few minutes later she lets out another one, right in his face.

The fellow jumps up and says, "This sure feels good, but I don't think I can take sixty-seven more of those farts."

●

Why do women like to play Pac-Man?
  Because they can get eaten three times for a quarter.

●

What do you call a prostitute who douches with Pepsi?
  A Pop-Tart.

●

One day a certain housewife was going about the usual business of cleaning the house when she suddenly felt intensely horny. Unfortunately her husband was still at work, so she resorted to stripping off all her clothes and starting to masturbate. She got pretty excited, rubbing herself and moaning, and when her husband walked in she was writhing in the middle of the living-room floor. He looked through the mail and said to his wife, "Honey, when you're finished vacuuming the floor, could you get started on dinner?"

●

Why are most cowgirls bowlegged?

Because cowboys never take their hats off when they eat.

●

What was the most erotic thing ever said on TV?
"Gee, Ward, you were kind of rough on the Beaver last night."

●

Did you hear about the prostitute who had an appendectomy?
The doctor sewed up the wrong hole, so now she's making money on the side.

●

What did the vampire say to the teacher?
"See you next period."

●

The horny husband always seems to have a hard time convincing his wife to have sex. One night, just before climbing into bed, he hands her a glass of water and two aspirins.
"But I don't have a headache," she protested.
"Gotcha!"

●

Why don't girls wear dresses in the winter?
Chapped lips.

Why was the girl fired from the sperm bank after she got pregnant?

Her employers discovered that she'd been embezzling.

●

These three men went for a drive in the country and their car broke down, so they went to the nearest farmhouse to ask for shelter for the night. "Sure, fellas," said the farmer, "you can spend the night here, but you've each got to sleep with one of my daughters, 'cause they don't get much company out here." The men all agreed, and during the night the farmer got up to make sure they were going through with their part of the deal.

The next morning the men went on their way and the farmer called his daughters together. "Linda, why were you laughing last night?"

"Because it tickled, Daddy."

"Susie, why were you crying?"

"Because it hurt, Daddy."

"Lizzie, why was your room silent?"

"Because he told me not to talk with my mouth full."

●

A man said to a hooker, "What would your mother say if she saw you doing this?"

"She'd kill me: I'm on her corner."

●

Rule at the girls' school: lights out at ten, candles out at ten-thirty.

A college professor had a reputation for offending women in his anthropology classes, so a bunch of co-eds got together and agreed to walk out the next time it happened. The next week, while discussing an obscure African tribe, the professor leered and said, "The men over there have penises twelve inches long!"

The co-eds rose and headed for the door.

"Oh, come on, girls," snickered the professor, "the plane doesn't leave till Sunday."

•

What's the ultimate in punk?

A pubic Mohawk.

•

How do you make a hormone?

Put sawdust in the Vaseline.

•

A nice young girl finally made an appointment with a certain Dr. Silva and asked, "Is it true you can make things grow?" The doctor assured her that it was true, and she blurted out, "Please give me something to make my tits grow: I can't stand being so flat-chested anymore."

"Easy enough," said Dr. Silva. "You must say 'Mary had a little lamb' three times a day."

On her way home she went to the supermarket. In the frozen-foods aisle, after looking both ways to make sure she was alone, she said quickly, "Mary had a little lamb" and then prayed to God. Suddenly a man stepped out from behind her and said, "I see you've been to Dr. Silva too."

"Why, yes," she stammered. "How did you know?"

He pulled down his zipper and reached for his cock, shouting, "*Hickory dickory dock!*"

●

How can you tell when a girl is horny?

When you put your hand down her pants and it feels like a horse eating oats.

●

What do you call the area between the vagina and the asshole?

A chin rest.

●

What are three things a woman can do that a man can't?
(1) Have a baby.
(2) Have her period.
(3) Get laid when she's dead.

●

Did you hear about the two sailors and the nurse who were stranded together on a desert island?

After three months the nurse was so disgusted with what she was doing that she killed herself.

After three more months the sailors were so disgusted with what they were doing that they buried her.

●

What's the difference between a young whore and an old whore?

A young whore uses Vaseline and an old whore uses Poli-Grip.

●

Hungry after overseeing the delivery of his cattle to a Chicago stockyard, a cowboy headed to a nearby restaurant for dinner. The only vacant seat was next to a young, wealthy, and well-educated young lady, and the cowboy couldn't help overhearing her place her order: "I'll have breast of fowl—virgin fowl. Make sure it's a virgin: Catch it yourself. Garnish my plate with onions and bring me a cup of coffee, not too hot and not too cold. Oh, and, waiter, open the window: I smell horse; there must be a cowboy in the house."

Thoroughly pissed off, the cowboy proceeded to place his own order: "I'll have duck—fucked duck: Fuck it yourself. Garnish my plate with horseshit, then bring me a cup of coffee as strong as Texas mule piss, and blow the foam off with a fart. Oh, and, waiter, knock down the wall: I smell cunt; there must be a whore in the house."

●

What's the ultimate embarrassment for a woman?

Taking her German shepherd to the vet and finding out he has the clap.

●

How many animals can you find in a pair of pantyhose?

Two calves; ten little piggies; one ass; one pussy; one thousand hares; maybe some crabs; and a dead fish nobody can find.

A mother and a daughter lived together in devastating poverty, so it was cause for great rejoicing when, on her way home from school, the daughter found fifty cents on the sidewalk. She ran home and showed it to her mother, who decided that for fifty cents they could get two eggs and a bottle of ketchup and have a real meal. So off went the daughter to the store.

As luck would have it, the daughter was happily skipping home with the eggs and ketchup when a truck backfired, startling her so much that she dropped the groceries. Staring down at the ruined feast, which was smashed at her feet, she sat down and started to cry.

A man came up behind her and surveyed the scene for a few moments. "There there, honey, don't cry," he said consolingly, "It would have died anyway: Its eyes were too far apart."

●

Why is a clitoris like Antarctica?
Most men know it's there, but few really care.

●

What's the best thing about Women's Liberation?
It gives you girls something to do in your spare time!

●

A young lady walks into a drugstore and asks the pharmacist for a gross of rubbers. Thinking that an order of that magnitude deserves a snappy answer, the pharmacist asks what size she would like.

"Oh, mix them up," she replies. "I'm not going steady."

A good-looking woman walks into a bar and orders a Michelob Light. It tastes so good that she orders another, and another, and another, until she passes out cold. Several truck drivers have been watching this progression of events with interest, and promptly take her into the back room and energetically screw her. Early the next morning the woman comes to and goes home, but that night she appears again, orders a Michelob Light, and gets so drunk that the truck drivers have their way with her again. This goes on for several more nights until one evening, when the woman shows up and orders a Miller Lite. Recognizing her, the bartender inquires as to why she's switched beers.

She replies, "Oh, Michelob makes my pussy hurt."

•

An employee of a factory that makes all sorts of rubber goods, from tires to rubber bands, was giving some guests a factory tour. Of special interest was the condom plant, where rubbers were being peeled off cock-shaped molds and rolled up for packaging. But every twelfth one was shuttled aside and a small hole was punched in it. Shocked, one of the visitors exclaimed, "What are you doing? Think of all the unwanted pregnancies that's going to cause!"

"Yeah," said the employee, "but it sure helps the nipple division."

•

Sadly neglected by her husband, a horny housewife turned to her next-door neighbor for advice. "Why don't you order your milk from the milkman" was the suggestion, "and when the bill comes, see if you can settle it with sex." This seemed like an excellent idea, and sure enough, when the bill was presented, the milkman was delighted to settle for a long and energetic screw. Putting his pants back on, the milkman reached for the bill to mark it "Paid in Full."

"Oh, no you don't," said the housewife, grabbing the bill. "You brought me this milk a quart at a time, and that's the way I'm gonna pay for it."

●

After going through Lamaze, Leboyer, and La Leche classes with his expectant wife, the proud new father remained by his wife's bedside throughout labor and birth, bonding with the newborn child. Wanting to be as sympathetic as possible, he took his wife's hand and said emotionally, "Tell me how it was, darling, tell me how it actually felt to give birth."

His wife replied, "Sure. Smile as hard as you can."

Beaming down beatifically at his wife and child, the father said, "That's not too hard."

She continued, "Now insert your index fingers into the corners of your mouth." He obeyed, still smiling broadly.

"Now stretch your lips as far as it will go. . . ."

"Still not too tough," he commented.

"Right," she retorted. "Now pull them over your head."

●

Heard about the virginity restoration kit?

A needle, a thread, and a maraschino cherry.

●

"When my husband climaxes," the woman complained to the marriage counselor, "his reaction includes an ear-shattering yell."

"All things considered," commented the counselor, "I should think that might be a certain source of satisfaction for you."

"Oh it would be," she said, "if it just didn't wake me up!"

•

Taken the Sex Quiz yet? Answer each question "True" or "False." Time limit: two hours.

(1) A clitoris is a type of flower.
(2) A pubic hair is a wild rabbit.
(3) A vulva is a Swedish automobile.
(4) A spread eagle is an extinct bird.
(5) A fallopian tube is a part inside a TV.
(6) A wet dream is dangerous if you sleep under an electric blanket.
(7) McDonald's golden arches are phallic symbols.
(8) A vagina is a medical term used to describe heart trouble.
(9) Fellatio is an Italian dagger.
(10) A menstrual cycle has three wheels.
(11) A G-string is a weapon used by G-men.
(12) *Semen* is a term for sailors.
(13) *Anus* is a Latin word denoting a long period of time.
(14) Testicles can be found on an octopus.
(15) Cunnilingus is a person who can speak four languages.
(16) *Asphalt* is a medical term for a rectal problem.
(17) KOTEX is a radio station in Dallas.
(18) Masturbate is something used to catch large fish.
(19) Coitus is a musical instrument.
(20) Fetus is a character on *Gunsmoke*.
(21) An umbilical cord is part of a parachute.
(22) A condom is an apartment complex.
(23) A rectum is what you are for doing this test!

82

Homosexuals

What kind of soup do they serve in a gay Chinese restaurant?
  Cream of Some Young Guy.

•

Why does it take two gay men to rape a girl?
  One holds her down while the other does her hair.

•

What do you call a vampire in drag?
  A transvestbite.

•

Did you hear about the new NFL franchise consisting of an all-queer roster?
  They plan to be a real come-from-behind team.

What's the definition of dried fruit?
A homosexual with a vasectomy.

•

What do lesbians do for dinner?
Eat out.

•

A crowd gathered around the wreck of a truck carrying designer gowns and accessories. Then from the back of the crowd came a hysterical voice, "Please, please let me through: I'm a transvestite."

•

Why do airline pilots really like landing in San Francisco?
All they have to do is get the plane near the airport and they get sucked in.

•

How many straight San Francisco waiters does it take to change a light bulb?
Both of them.

•

A hot and dusty cowboy came into a bar, pounded his fist to get the bartender's attention, and said, "I'm so thirsty I could lick the sweat off a cow's balls!"
A fag sitting in the corner overheard and piped up with "Moo, moooo."

What does your typical homosexual use for the temporary
relief of minor arthritis?
  Ben-Gay.

●

What do you call a homosexual community in Alaska?
  Frosted flakes.

●

Why do men have nipples?
  So homosexuals will know what they're missing.

●

What's brown and squishy and wears pearls?
  The Gay Rights Movement.

●

And now for the latest AIDS jokes:

What's the difference between herpes and AIDS?
  One's a love story and the other's a fairy tale.

●

How do faggots spell relief?
  N-O-A-I-D-S.

●

What's sickle-cell anemia?
  AIDS for spades.

Did you hear about the new line of appliances for gays?
   They're called kitchen AIDS.

•

How do gays get into college?
   Financial AIDS.

•

What do you call a queer who doesn't have AIDS?
   A lucky cocksucker.

•

What do you call the gay Ice Follies?
   AIDS on blades.

•

What does *AIDS* stand for?
   Adiós, Infected Dick Sucker.

•

Why is AIDS a miracle?
   It's the only thing in the world that can change a fruit into a vegetable.

•

What happens if you get on a bus full of queers?
   You get off.

What do you get when you have 100 sex-crazed gays in the same room?

About a quart.

●

What was the gay cadet's defense when he was kicked out of the military college?

"They wouldn't have caught me if I hadn't attempted to switch majors."

●

What do queers call a rubber?

Seal-a-meal.

●

What's green, gay, and flies through the air?

Peter Pansy!

●

What did the constipated gay say to his boyfriend?

"With friends like you, who needs enemas?"

●

What do faggots do every twenty-eight days?

Stick a tampon up their assholes.

●

What does a lesbian get every twenty-eight days?

A free meal.

In a recent survey on why some men are homosexual, 82 percent of the men surveyed responded that either genetics or home environment was the principal factor. The remaining 18 percent revealed that they had been sucked into it.

●

What do you call a gay Smurf?
  A Smaggot.

●

A gay man paid a visit to his doctor and confided that he had a vibrator stuck up his ass. "Let me have a look," said the doctor reassuringly. "I'll have it out in no time."
  "Oh, doctor, please don't do that," said the gay.
  "What the hell do you want me to do?" asked the doctor.
  "Change the batteries, please."

●

Farmer Jones died during the winter, and when it came time for spring planting, Widow Jones realized she couldn't do all the work herself. So she applied to the town council, only to be told that all the able-bodied farmhands had already been hired and the only two left were an ex-con and a queer. Widow Jones chose the queer, and was pleased to find him a steady and reliable worker. When six weeks of hard labor had gone by, the man asked Widow Jones if he could have Saturday night off to go into town. "All right," she consented, "but be back by nine o'clock."
  The farmhand wasn't back until ten-thirty, and as he tiptoed up the stairs he heard Widow Jones summon him to her room. "Take off my shoes," she commanded. He

obeyed. "Take off my dress." He did so." "Take off my slip . . . and my stockings . . . and my garter belt."

The queer obeyed without saying a word.

"Now take off my bra," snapped Widow Jones, "and don't you ever borrow my clothes again!"

Religious

What do you call a gay nun?
  A transister.

•

A little boy was throwing a temper tantrum on a crowded sidewalk when an elderly minister walked by. Stopping the flustered mother with an upraised hand, he bent down and whispered something in the child's ear. Instantly the child calmed, stood up, and returned docilely to his mother's side, and the bystander burst into a smattering of applause. One took the minister by the sleeve and asked, "Excuse me, Reverend, but what magic words *did* you use on that little boy?"

  The old man smiled and gently said, "I told him that if he didn't get the hell off the sidewalk, I'd kick his fucking ass to the moon."

•

Later that day the little boy had another fit on a crowded sidewalk, and this time it was a retired priest whose whispered words calmed the hysterical child. When asked what he had said, the priest smiled sweetly and explained, "I held up my big silver crucifix and said, 'See that man? He used to misbehave in public places too.'"

●

Did you hear about Jesus Christ walking into a hotel in Galilee, slapping three nails down on the desk, and asking, "Could you put me up for the night?"

●

One fine day a rabbi, a minister, and a priest rent a rowboat and go fishing in a nearby lake. Pretty soon the reverend says, "If you'll excuse me, nature calls," gets out of the boat, and walks across the water to a privy on the shore. A few minutes after he rejoins the fishing party in the same manner, the priest excuses himself for the same reason, walks across the water to the privy, and returns nice and dry to the boat. The rabbi marvels at this, wondering if they have special God-given powers, and as his own bladder fills up he wonders if he might not have some special powers himself. So he stands up and excuses himself, steps overboard, and sinks like a stone. Splashing and struggling to the surface, the rabbi yells, "Help me, O God, help me!"

The minister and the priest look at each other, and the priest says, "Should we tell him about the rocks?"

●

What do nuns and Seven-Up have in common?
Never had it, never will.

A new building was going up next door to the convent and the sisters' devotions were constantly being interrupted by the foul language used by the construction workers. Unable to stand it any longer, the Mother Superior went next door and asked to speak to the foreman. After listening to her complaint, the foreman said, "I'm sorry, Sister, but we believe in calling a spade a spade."

"The heck you do," said the Mother Superior. "You call it a fucking shovel."

●

Joseph and Mary were riding their donkeys to Bethlehem when Mary's slipped and they tumbled down the bank. Joseph ran over to the edge, saw Mary lying dazed below, and called out, "Mary, are you all right?"

"I think so" was her feeble answer, "but I don't know if the baby is."

"Never mind that," said Joseph. "We don't know who the father is anyway."

●

What do a Christmas tree and a priest have in common?
    They both have balls just for decoration.

●

A nun was killing some time in the airport before her plane left so she put her penny into a weight-and-fortune machine, stood on the scale, and waited for the card to come out. It read: "You are a Catholic nun; your height is 5′5″; your weight is 150 lbs.; and you are about to expel gas." She couldn't believe this, but sure enough, about ten minutes later, she felt a terrific pain in her gut and had to run for the ladies room to fart discreetly. Amazed, she returned to the machine, inserted another penny, and got a card that read: "You are a Catholic nun; you are 5'5"; you weigh 150 lbs.; and you are going to be raped." Sure enough, as she stepped down from the scale a man grabbed her, dragged her off to the men's room, and raped her. Staggering out of the men's room, she climbed back on the scale, inserted another penny, and got a card that read: "You are 5'5"; you weigh 150 lbs.; and you have farted and fucked around and missed your plane."

●

What did God say to Jesus Christ?
  "I don't care if you are my son: Drop that cross once more and you're out of the parade."

●

Sister Bridget was asking her third-grade class what each of them would like to be when they grew up. Little Mary said, "I'd like to be a nurse." Young Michael said, "I want to be a policeman." Little Nora said, "I want to be a prostitute!"
  Sister Bridget fainted dead away. Upon being revived, she asked again what little Nora had said, and when she was told, a smile came over her face. "Thanks be to God," said the sister, "I thought she said a *Protestant*."

●

What do you get when you cross nuns and chickens?
  A pecking order.

●

What did the centurion say to Jesus Christ?
  "Cross your legs: We only have three nails."

93

Every time Timmy's mom has her boyfriend over, she puts Timmy in the closet with his teddy bear. One day, hearing her husband coming up the stairs, she shoves her boyfriend into the closet with Timmy.

"Gee, it's mighty dark in here," says Timmy.

The boyfriend replies, "Yeah, it sure is."

"You wanna buy my teddy bear for fifty bucks?" asks Timmy.

"No way, kid, you're crazy," says the boyfriend.

"I'll scream," says Timmy.

So the boyfriend forks over the money, and the next time Grandma comes over she notices that he's spending money like crazy on toys and comic books. "Where'd you get the money to buy all those things?" she asks, but Timmy isn't about to tell. "Well, if you won't tell me, you'll have to go to confession and tell the priest," says Grandma, and drags him off to the church. Timmy enters the gloomy confession booth and says, "Gee, it's dark in here."

And the priest says, "Are you gonna start that shit again?"

•

How do you get a nun pregnant?
Screw her.

•

One day not too long ago, God decided He was overdue for a vacation. "I hear Mars is nice," suggested St. Peter.

"Not again," said God. "I'm still sore from the sunburn I got there 10,000 years ago."

"I had a good time on Pluto," piped up the Archangel Gabriel.

"No way," said God. "I nearly broke my neck 5,000 years ago skiing there."

94

"There's always Earth," spoke up a small seraph.

"Are you nuts?" shouted God. "I dropped by there 2,000 years ago and I'm still in trouble for knocking up some Jewish chick."

Old Age

Two elderly men sitting around the senior citizens' center on a Sunday, catching up on each other's affairs. "So, Herb, how's it going?" asked Larry. "Are you getting any?"

Herb replied, "Almost every night, I'm telling you."

"At your age? I don't mean to be disrespectful, Herb, but I just don't believe it."

Said Herb, "It's true. Almost Monday night, almost Tuesday night, almost Wednesday night . . ."

●

Why is a woman over sixty like Australia?

Everyone knows it's down under, but who gives a damn?

●

An old man and his wife were sitting on their porch one warm summer afternoon, listening to a healing preacher on their favorite radio station. The preacher said, "Now, I want you to put your hand on the part of your body that most needs some healing, and we will pray together for its return to health.'' So the old woman put her hand over her heart, hoping the prayers would make it stronger. Her husband looked over slyly to make sure she wasn't looking, then snuck his hand down to his crotch. His wife looked over and says, "Harold, the preacher said he was going to heal the part, not raise the dead!"

•

Milton was getting on in years—he was well into his eighties—and decided it was time for a last fling. So he went out and hired himself a prostitute for a last night of pleasure.

About three weeks later he felt a growing pain in his groin and rushed over to the doctor's office, insisting on an emergency consultation. The doctor examined him thoroughly, then asked if he could ask a personal question. "Have you been with a woman anytime recently?"

Milton confessed the truth.

"Well, you better go look her up right away, 'cause you're about to come!"

•

Sam and Sally were virgins when they were married and so embarrassed about the sex act that they agreed to refer to it as "doing the laundry." Fifty years later their prudery had not diminished, but every so often Sam would get his hopes up and ask if he could put something in the washing machine. "Maybe in a little while, Sam," Sally answered one cold night as they tottered into the bedroom.

Under the covers he poked her in the ribs and asked, "How about a little laundry, honey?"

No answer from Sally, but about ten minutes later, having thought it over, she whispered, "Okay, Sam, the washing machine's ready."

"Aw, gee, honey," he quavered, "it was just a small load, I did it by hand."

●

Did you hear about the ninety-two-year-old man who was arrested for attempted rape of a seventeen-year-old high school girl?

The charge was "assault with a dead weapon."

●

This old guy and his wife have been spending the last thirty winters at the same Miami Beach resort, and for at least twenty of them the same prostitute's been regularly propositioning the old geezer; it's a pretty swank resort so she figures it'd be well worth her time. Finally, tired of fending her off after all these years, the guy gives in. "Okay," he says, "I'll go to bed with you. But since I retired, my wife handles the money, so is it okay if she comes too?"

●

What do you call an old Mexican woman?

A bean bag.

●

There was once a seventy-seven-year-old spinster who detected something nasty going on in her nether regions and, somewhat embarrassed, went to the doctor for tests. Sure enough, the doctor produced a diagnosis of crabs. "That's quite impossible," gasped the old woman. "I am seventy-seven and a virgin." Deciding to get a second opinion, she had another doctor do a checkup, but he only confirmed the unfortunate diagnosis. "How can that be?" she stammered. "In seventy-seven years no man has ever touched me." And off she went to the hospital for an enormous battery of tests. Eventually a young doctor came into her room and announced that he had some good news and some bad news.

"Give me the good news first," asked the old woman.

"You don't have crabs," said the doctor. "The bad news is that your cherry has rotted and you have fruit flies."

●

Two old ladies are sitting in their rocking chairs at the nursing home, reminiscing. One turns to the other and says, "Mildred, do you remember the minuet?"

"Good heavens, no," replies Mildred, "I don't even remember the ones I screwed."

Miscellaneous

An attorney was defending his client against a charge of first-degree murder. "Your Honor, my client is accused of stuffing his lover's mutilated body into a suitcase and heading for the Mexican border. Just north of Tijuana a cop spotted her hand sticking out of the suitcase.

"Now, I would like to stress that my client is *not* a murderer. A sloppy packer, maybe . . ."

●

Why are there no jokes about the Jonestown tragedy?
Because the punch line's too long.

●

What's the difference between a Rolls Royce and a Valley Girl?
Not everyone's been in a Rolls Royce.

●

After this fellow was through at the local whorehouse, the prostitute looked up from the bed and simpered, "What do you want to name the child?'' The man thought this was a bit presumptuous and walked out, thoroughly pissed off. He came back for more a few weeks later and was even angrier when the question was asked a second time. Quickly taking off his rubber, he tied it in a knot, tossed it out the window, and said, ''If he can get out of that, I'll call him Houdini.''

●

One day a man was sunbathing on a nude beach when he noticed a little girl staring down at him, so he put a newspaper over his private parts. The girl asked him what that was, and he explained that it was his bird and that he kept it under there so it wouldn't fly away. He fell asleep, and when he woke up he found himself in a hospital room. ''What happened?'' he asked.

The little girl stepped in and said, ''While you were sleeping I wanted to play with your bird. But it spit at me, so I broke its neck, crushed its eggs, and set its nest on fire.''

●

There's a rumor that some independent skin-flick producers are combining to form a major studio.

It's going to be called Twentieth Century-Fux.

●

Little Joey wins a big bag of M & M's at the carnival and runs home to show his mom. He begs for some and his mother gives him two. Joey pops them in his mouth, runs outside, bites the cat, and jumps on his tricycle to boogie around the house. Coming to a screeching halt in front, he runs inside, grabs two more M & M's, pops them in his mouth, runs outside, bites the cat, and races around the house on his tricycle. This is repeated a few more times until his mother asks him what in heaven's name he is up to.

"I'm playing truck driver, Mom," he explains. "I'm popping pills, eating pussy, and driving like hell."

●

Hear about Snow White's swingin' party?
   She woke up feeling Dopey.

●

What's worse than being pissed off?
   Being pissed on.

●

What do you call a sexual aid for hobbyists?
   A Heath-clit.

●

Jack was getting onto his commuter train when he heard a man standing on the platform yelling to a guy inside the train, "Your wife is a great fuck! Your wife is fantastic in bed!" Surprised and a little curious, Jack went over to the guy who was doing the yelling and asked him why he'd want to say such a thing in public.

The guy shrugged. "Well, actually she's a lousy lay, but I didn't want to hurt his feelings."

•

The third-grade teacher was teaching English and repeated for her class: "Mary had a little lamb, whose fleece was white as snow/And everywhere that Mary went, the lamb was sure to go." She explained that this was an example of poetry, but could be changed to prose by changing the last line from "the lamb was sure to go" to "the lamb went with her."

A few days later she asked for an example of poetry or prose. Johnny raised his hand and recited, "Mary had a little pig, an ornery little runt/He stuck his nose in Mary's clothes, and smelled her little—" He stopped and asked the teacher if she wanted poetry or prose.

"Prose," the teacher said weakly.

So Johnny said, "Asshole."

•

Three door-to-door vacuum-cleaner salesmen show up at a farmhouse one afternoon, and the kindly farmer agrees to buy a vacuum from each if they'll keep their hands off his virginal daughter while he's at the bank, getting the money. But when he gets back he finds all three on top of his daughter. Irate, he fires a shotgun blast over their heads, marches them out to the garden, and tells them each to pick ten of any fruit or vegetable.

The first salesman comes forward with ten peas. "Shove them up your ass," orders the farmer. The second guy turns up with ten tomatoes and gets the same order. He has some trouble getting them up his ass, especially as he keeps cracking up. but finally gets the job done. "You're free to go," the farmer says to him, "but do you mind if I ask what's so damn funny?"

Collapsing with laughter once again, the salesman says, "The third guy's still out there, picking watermelons."

●

When does a Cub Scout become a Boy Scout?
    When he eats his first Brownie.

●

A man was admitted to the hospital for emergency plastic surgery on his penis. After he came to, the surgeon dropped by and said, "Excuse my curiosity, but I've never seen injuries like yours; how did it happen?"

"Well, doc," said the patient, "I live in a camper, and right next door's another camper that belongs to this really hot chick. Every night I spy on her, and what she does is stick a hot dog in a hole in the floor, strip, and start fucking it. Well, one night I can't take it anymore and I get a bright idea. I crawl under her camper and stick my dick through the hole where the hot dog goes. I was having a great time until someone knocked on the door and she started kicking the hot dog under the stove."

●

Batman and Superman were assigned to a crime-watch patrol one day, and Batman noticed that Superman's clothes were torn and his face bruised. So he asked what had happened. Superman replied, "I was flying home one day when I spotted Batwoman sunbathing nude on her rooftop. I didn't want to give her a chance to run for her clothes, so I snuck up from behind and jumped on top of her."

"Was she surprised?" asked Batman.

"Not half as surprised as the Invisible Man."

What's a 6.9?
   A 69 interrupted by a period.

●

What's a 72?
   A 69 with 5-percent meal tax.

●

How do you make a dead baby float?
   You take your foot off its head and let it rise to the surface.

●

What's more fun than shoveling dead babies off the sidewalk?
   Using a snow-blower.

●

What's worse than finding ten dead babies in a trash can?
   Finding one dead baby in ten trash cans.

●

How did the couple into S&M have fun in their car?
   They used the cigarette lighter.

●

What's Smurf sex?
   Fucking till you're blue in the face.

When his company fell on hard times, the boss realized he'd have to lay off one of his two middle managers, although both Jack and Jill were equally honest and dedicated to their jobs. Unable to decide which to fire, the boss arbitrarily decided that the first to leave his or her desk the next morning would be the one to get the ax.

The next morning found Jill at her desk, rubbing her temples. Asking Jack for some aspirin, she headed for the water fountain and that's where the boss caught up with her. "I've got some news for you, Jill," he said. "I'm going to have to lay you or Jack off."

"Jack off," she snapped. "I have a headache."

•

"Mommy, Mommy, have you seen my Cabbage Patch doll?"

"Shut up and eat your cole slaw."

•

How can you tell if you have an overbite?

If you're eating pussy and it tastes like shit.

•

Little Jimmy was driving his mother nuts, so finally she said, "Why don't you go across the street and watch the men building the new house. Maybe you'll learn something." When Jimmy came back in at suppertime, his mother asked him what he'd learned. "First you put the goddamned door up," said little Jimmy sweetly, "and then the son of a bitch doesn't fit, so you take the cocksucker down. So you take a cunt hair off each side and then put the motherfucker back up."

Shocked, Jimmy's mother said, "You're going to have

106

a talk with your dad tonight." When Jimmy's father came in, she said, "Tell Daddy what you learned today, Jimmy." The kid repeated his lesson in carpentry. "Jimmy, go get a switch," bellowed his angry father.

Jimmy replied, "Fuck you, that's the electrician's job."

Mary Jane Jokes

Mary Jane went to the drive-in with her boyfriend one night and he started to make advances, putting his hand down her bra.

Mary Jane laughed and she laughed and she laughed . . . because she knew that her money was in her sock.

●

Mary Jane went to the doctor one day. The doctor came out and said, "Mary Jane I have some news for you: You're pregnant *and* you're going to have twins!"

Mary Jane laughed and she laughed and she laughed . . . because she knew that she'd only done it once.

●

Mary Jane was in the living room reading a book. Her dad came in, ripped the book from her hands, and threw it across the room.

Mary Jane laughed and she laughed and she laughed . . . because she knew what page she was on.

Mary Jane went into the house screaming, "Mommy, Mommy! I just set the garage on fire!" Her mother said, "Mary Jane, your father is going to kill you."

Mary Jane laughed and she laughed and she laughed . . . because she knew her dad was in the garage.

Too Tasteless to Be Included

What's the difference between a dead dog in the road and a dead black in the road?

There's skid marks in front of the dog.

●

What's worse than Jimmy Durante with a bloody nose?

Dolly Parton with breast cancer.

●

There is a young woman who, instead of disposing of her tampons normally, throws them into her closet. One day she is entertaining her lover when she hears the front door open, so she quickly hides him in the closet and locks the door. It's her husband surprising her with two tickets for a weekend in Hawaii, and in her excitement she forgets all about her lover and dashes off to Hawaii. On Monday she waits till her husband has gone off to work and opens the closet door, expecting the worse. But he's in fine shape and says cheerfully, "Hell, if it weren't for all those

110

jelly doughnuts you had in there, I never would have made it!''

•

Why are there no black people in Wisconsin?
  The Indians think they taste like venison.

•

What does the blinking neon sign above Joe's 24-hour Abortion Clinic say?
  YOU RAPE 'EM. WE SCRAPE 'EM.

•

What's the difference between a Biafran baby and an NFL football?
  The football has to weigh at least fourteen ounces.

•

Two old bums are walking along the railroad tracks, starving, because they haven't eaten in three days. Coming across a dead and mangled cat, the first bum says, "Oh, boy— lunch!" He digs in, stopping only to ask his friend if he wants some. "No, thanks, I think I'll pass" is the answer. So the first bum devours the whole cat, leaving nothing behind but fur and bones, and they continue their walk down the tracks. About a mile later the first bum turns green and throws up the whole cat. All excited, his companion says happily, "That's what I've been waiting for—a hot lunch!"

What did the southern governor say about the holiday for Martin Luther King?

"Shoot four more and we'll take a week off."

●

What do you get when you cross Sister Theresa with a black prostitute?

The Black Hole of Calcutta.

●

A guy went to the whorehouse and the madam asked him what sort of activities he preferred. "I have a certain, uh, idiosyncrasy," he admitted.

"Our girls are used to anything," said the madam reassuringly. "Betty, take this gentleman upstairs." Five minutes later there's a piercing scream and Betty comes running down the stairs, followed soon after by the dejected man. The madam insists on knowing just what it is his tastes run to, and finally the guy confesses, "I like to have the broad lay on the floor while I shit on her stomach." The madam says, "Why didn't you say so? Alice is the girl for you." So he goes upstairs with Alice, everything goes according to plan, and the guy enjoys himself so much that he goes back the next night to see Alice and becomes a regular customer, stopping by three or four times a week.

One night he's horny but terrifically constipated, and he goes over to the whorehouse for Alice. They go upstairs and he squats on top of her. But despite massive straining and groaning, he can only manage a tiny fart. At which Alice breaks into heartbreaking sobs. "What's the matter?" he asks, turning around.

Tears running down her cheeks, she weeps, "You don't love me anymore."

What's grosser than gross?
　Two vampires fighting over a used tampon.

●

What's grosser than gross?
　When a guy fingers a girl and pulls out someone else's class ring.
What's even grosser?
　When a cheerleader does the splits and two rings falls out: One's her boyfriend's and one's her own.

●

What's grosser than gross?
　Running over a baby in a Mack truck.
What's grosser than that?
　Skidding on it.
What's even grosser than that?
　Peeling it off the tire.

●

What's the different between rude and crude?
　Rude is when you throw your underwear against the wall and crude is when it sticks.

●

After a long and difficult delivery, the obstetrician finally pulled the baby out, whirled it around over his head, and let go so that it splattered all over the wall. "Doctor!" shrieked the woman. "That was my baby!"
　"That's okay. It was dead anyhow."

The victim of an awful automobile accident was pronounced dead on arrival at the hospital, and the emergency-room nurse was instructed to prepare the body for the undertaker. Removing his bloody clothes, she discovered that the young man had died with the most massive erection she had ever seen. Unable to take her eyes of it, she finally yielded to temptation, took off her panties, straddled the stiff, and proceeded to enjoy herself. She was getting down from the table when a second nurse came in and reprimanded her for her obscene behavior. "What's the harm?" shot back the first nurse. "I enjoyed it, and he surely didn't mind it. Besides, he can't complain and I can't get pregnant. Why don't you give it a try."

"Oh, I couldn't possibly," said the second nurse, blushing. "First, he's dead, and second, I've got my period. Listen, the doctor wants you in the operating room, and I'm supposed to finish up in here." She got to work, but soon found herself terribly excited by this massive hard-on and climbed on top of it. Just as she was starting to come, she was astonished to feel the man climax too. Looking down and seeing his eyelids starting to flutter, she exclaimed, "I thought you were dead!"

"I thought I was, too, lady," said the man, "until you gave me that blood transfusion."

●

Why do you wrap a hamster in electrician's tape?
    So it won't explode when you fuck it.

●

What do you do with a dead black?
    Scalp him and use the hair as a Brillo pad.

114

The fourteen-year-old boy was making love to his twelve-year-old sister. "Geez, Sis," he wheezes, "you're almost as good as Maw!"

"Yeah," she gasps back, "that's what Paw says."

●

Why do convents always take in abandoned babies?
Because they can be made into communion wafers.

●

How can you tell if a fence is electrified?
Throw a puppy at it and see if he gets fried.

●

Southern politician: "I have nothing against blacks; I think everyone should own one."

●

What do you call a prostitute with a runny nose?
Full.

●

How many Karen Carpenter's does it take to change a light bulb?
It depends on how you stack the bones.

Would you like to see your favorite tasteless jokes in print? If so, send them to:

Blanche Knott
c/o St. Martin's Press
175 Fifth Avenue
New York, N.Y. 10010

PLUS

Having problems that may be too tasteless or too bizarre for your average advice columnist? Write c/o DEAR BLANCHE at the above address, and keep an eye out for DEAR BLANCHE: ADVICE FOR THE EIGHTIES, in your bookstore next year.

Remember, we're sorry but no compensation or credit can be given.